Stefan Luckhaus

Book Series
Increasing Productivity of Software Development

Part 1
# Productivity and Performance Measurement – Measurability and Methods

Internet: www.pass-consulting.com

Editing & Proofreading:
Heidrun Fernau-Rienecker, Anelka Dudaczy

Cover Design & Typesetting:
Antje Schwarzbauer

Cover Graphic & Photos:
Shutterstock Images LLC

Production & Distribution:
PASS IT-Consulting Dipl. Inf. G. Rienecker GmbH & Co. KG
Heidrun Fernau-Rienecker

Print:
tredition

Printed in Germany
March 2018


ISBN:
Hardcover:   978-3-9819565-6-6
Paperback:   978-3-9819565-8-0
e-Book:      978-3-9819565-7-3

# Contents

# Contents

| | |
|---|---|
| Contents | 4 |
| Figures | 8 |
| Tables | 10 |
| Preface | 13 |
| Motivation | 14 |
| Future-shaper ICT | 14 |
| The objectives of this book series | 16 |
| About this book | 17 |
| I. Introduction | 19 |
| The key to a global innovation competition | 20 |
| Software drives innovations | 21 |
| II. The Evolution of IT | 23 |
| IT penetrates enterprises | 24 |
| The use of information technology from 1960 to 2015 | 27 |
| 1960 to 1969 | 27 |
| 1970 to 1979 | 28 |
| 1980 to 1989 | 29 |
| 1990 to 1999 | 30 |
| 2000 to 2009 | 32 |
| 2010 bis 2019 | 34 |

What could the future look like? 36

The importance of productive software development 40

## III. What is Productivity and how can it be measured? 43

Different aspects of productivity 44

Productivity of software development 46

Requirement 1: Process scope is defined consistent 46

Requirement 2: Final product quality is consistently 47

Requirement 3: Input is measurable 47

Requirement 4: Output is measurable 48

## IV. Methods for measuring the Development Output 51

Requirements on a size metric 52

Code metrics 54

Functional size measurement 55

Function Point Analysis 58

The COSMIC Method 63

The Data Interaction Point Method 67

Comparison of measurement methods 71

More measuring methods 76

## V. Automation and the Limits of Measurability    79

Measurements are a cross-sectional task    80
Approaches for automated measurements    80
Potential inaccuracies when measuring implemented systems    81

## VI. The Impact of Complexity    85

The complexity of implemented code    86
Interactional complexity    88
Algorithmic complexity    90

## VII. Tips and Hints for a practical Introduction    93

Definition of objectives    94
Stage 1: Evaluation and calibration of a measuring method    95
Stage 2: Launch and collection of empirical values    96
Stage 3: The practical use of measurements    97

## VIII. Conclusion    101

## Glossary    104

## Bibliography    120

## About the Author    124

## Book Recommendations    126

# Figures

Figure 1:     Value contributions of IT in enterprises                                          24

Figure 2:     Reference model for enterprises                                                    25

Figure 3:     The Kondratjev-Waves                                                               37

Figure 4:     Productivity from a business point of view                                         45

Figure 5:     Sample Use Case Diagram                                                            56

Figure 6:     Objects to be counted by the Function Point Analysis                               58

Figure 7:     Weighting matrices for elementary processes                                        60

Figure 8:     Weighting matrices for data structures                                             61

Figure 9:     Objects to be counted by the COSMIC Method                                         64

Figure 10:    Objects to be counted by the Data Interaction Point
              Method                                                                             68

Figure 11:    Comparison of size measurements of different systems
              by FPA, COSMIC and DIP                                                             71

Figure 12:    Sample program #1                                                                  87

Figure 13:    Sample Program #2                                                                  87

Figure 14:    Management Model for Increasing Productivity of
              Software Development                                                               99

# Tables

Table 1:     Sample BFCs of a Use Case                                          57

Table 2:     Functional Size of Sample Use Case „Search Flight"
             measured by FPA                                                    62

Table 3:     Functional Size of Sample Use Case „Search Flight"
             measured by COSMIC                                                 66

Table 4:     Functional Size of Sample Use Case „Search Flight"
             measured by DIP                                                    70

Table 5:     Comparison of FPA, COSMIC and DIP Method                          75

Table 6:     Objectives, requirements and benefits                             94

# Preface

to the Book Series

# Increasing Productivity
# of Software Development

Gerhard Rienecker

## Motivation

If you can answer the following questions with a clear "yes", this book series on productivity of software development cannot provide new ideas. Put down this book and pursue your objectives by means of your own strategies. However, if you cannot say "yes" beyond doubt or if you have a tendency to say "no", this book series can definitely be a source of inspiration.

Questions:

1) Is your IT shop managed by clear KPIs?
2) Do you know your productivity and quality performance?
3) Do you know the development productivity of your developers?
4) Do you know the maintenance efficiency of your developers?
5) Do you know the processing performance of your applications?

Well, you are still reading. I did not expect anything else. For more than 30 years I am an IT consultant, in business for many well-known companies and I must say that most of the IT organizations do not have answers to these questions. There are many initiatives and approaches, but most of them remain rudimentary. Continuous IT management strategies, which can answer the questions above clearly and consistently, are extremely scarce. I would appreciate your feedback.

## Future-shaper ICT

Since the invention of the first freely programmable computer in 1941 by Konrad Zuse, the information and communication technologies (ICTs) derived from it write one success story after another. ICT penetrates our lives more and more. It shapes and organizes business functions and processes and pursues the continuous IT-zation of businesses (real-time enterprises or internet companies). It makes many products smart (you can find more than 100 processors with a lot of software in a new car today). In the past, the omnipotence of ICT has led to revolutionary changes of products such as cameras, music players and media, mobile phones, and so on. More and more it contributes to the individual lifestyle, be it game consoles or movie creation, and it even revolutionizes entire industries. ICT has initiated the 5th Kondratiev wave [Korotayev/Tsirel 2010] – an economic cycle focusing on information as an economic asset and replacing the industrial society by the information society.

This economic asset is different from the goods of the industrial society. Information is intangible, has no natural scientific basis (physics, chemistry, and so on), cannot be explained by basic models, is not divisible, but it increases in social value if imparted (distributed). The significance of this asset will continue to increase along with the importance of ICT. I will not justify this statement, but I refer to some books presenting multiple evidence to this: **The Digital Enterprise** [Streibich 2014], **The New Digital Age** [Cohen/Schmidt 2013], **Vision 2030** [Meister 2012], **die 3. Industrielle Revolution** [Rifkin 2011], **Wem gehört die Zukunft?** [Lanier 2014] or even our last book **Quality, that's IT** [Rienecker et al 2011].

For the management of this economic asset 3 technologies are required: hardware technologies (CPU + memory), communication technologies and software technologies. Regarding software technologies we must differentiate between basic software (operating systems, middleware and database technologies) and application software. While for hardware and communication technologies the development of productivity follows Moore's law [Moore 1998], there is no reliable method for measuring the productivity development of software technologies. Particularly in the area of application software – where everybody can take notice of the values created by ICT, neither generally accepted methods nor practical procedures are available to measure performance or determine productivity increases. However, because ICT and particularly application software ever more advance to a future-shaper, the discrepancy between importance and controllability leads to an unsatisfactory situation. This is the motivation for this book series. Please let me reflect briefly on our objectives.

## The objectives of this book series

This book series targets the following objectives of organizations developing software:

- quality improvement,
- increase in productivity,
- improvement of the IT management model,
- improvement of performance measurement in the area of development, maintenance and production, and
- measuring performance on the basis of KPIs.

To achieve this objective we want to spend sufficient time and effort on every topic – in addition to the basic methods, concepts and strategies – to thereby enhance its transparency.

Currently we plan books on the following topics:

- Productivity and Performance Measurement, Measurability and Methods
- Cost Estimation and KPI-based Improvement
- Self-assessment and Optimization

- Quality Management

- KPA Application Specification

- KPA Application Architectures

- KPA System Architectures

- KPA Systems Operation

- KPA Development Architecture

- KPA Project Management

- KPA Human Resources Management

- Factories – from Manufacture to Software Production

## About this book

After a digression on the history of IT and an outlook on the possible future development this book initially describes the methodical basis of performance measurement. It compares the advantages and drawbacks of different measuring methods as well as the limits of measurability.

After a comparison of different methods which are available on the market we introduce our own method, the Data Interaction Point method, which has been developed by us 7 years ago and is the basis of our own management model.

According to our principle to only consult on topics where sufficient experience has been gained in-house, we can tell the inside story. Today, we use this methodology ourselves to manage more than 10 different application environments with more than 500 customers and over 250.000 users.

# I. Introduction

# The way to the global innovation competition

Since the beginning of the 1960s IT has changed our life continuously. Today, all areas of our life are more or less penetrated by IT. Many areas largely hinge on it. Banks, for example, would no longer be operable without it. Some enterprises are built on business models which even have been enabled by IT such as mobile phone service providers, virtual marketplaces, online auction houses, electronic pay services, and so on. Significant advancements have been made to integrate partners along the value chain, automate processes and virtualize products. This is reflected in the real-time trading of financial products when, for example, a loan requested in the internet will be paid off within seconds after a rule engine has calculated an appropriate rating. Due to IT, the industrial mass production today is capable of a high level of individual configuration. This becomes apparent when looking at the variant-richness of cars represented by configuration tools in the internet. At the same time an alternative to industrial production emerges: The consumer produces simple products himself by downloading a construction plan and using his 3D printer. The following chapter will describe this "evolution of IT" in detail.

Via the internet, enterprises can enter global markets, but the price to be paid is the loss of customer loyalty, a consequence of total transparency: as consumers can compare product specifications and performance data, prices, the online presentation of a shop, ratings by other customers, and so on. Thus, they buy per mouse click wherever it appeals to them most at this particular moment.

In consequence, more and more industries are faced with a global innovation and time-based competition. The time-based competition enables customers to notice any changes of the competitors' offerings immediately and therefore vendors, who want to remain competitive, are in a tight spot. The impact of the innovation competition is that vendors can stand out from run-of-the-mill only by innovations: innovative ideas requiring IT solutions with increasing complexity and created in less and less implementation time. Given this gap, only enterprises who can put their new, complex and yet attractive IT solutions on the market (to the internet) quickly and reliably, can be successful. Those who roughly estimate the effort of their IT projects and therefore are not able to plan reliably, who permanently postpone their delivery milestones or, driven by deadlines, accept quality deficiencies, will not succeed.

## Software drives innovations

IT systems are an interaction of hardware and software. Konrad Zuse built one of the world's first operable and freely programmable computers in 1941. He supposedly assumed that development and sale of hardware is a very lucrative business area whereas no money can be earned with software. However, he realized the importance of software for the sale of computers and their use in a growing number of areas. With "Plankalkül" he invented the first higher-level programming language which allowed a faster development of complex programs than using machine language [Alex 1997]. Konrad Zuse was wrong regarding the commercial potential of software, but his assessment of the relevance of software and the quick availability of new programs was correct and is more topical than ever today. Hardware is standardized, replaceable, scalable and networkable. Software, however maps our processes and complex rule sets, virtualizes and thus drives more innovations than hardware.

# II. The Evolution of IT

## IT penetrates enterprises

Figure 1 shows how the increased use of IT in companies can lead to value contributions. Companies, which are managed without IT, can generally only reach customers who are close to their place of business. Their major competitive advantage is their location and they primarily serve customers coming to their branches and paying cash. Examples are local craft businesses, small grocery stores or gastronomy sites in rural regions.

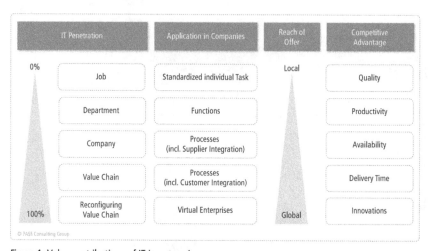

Figure 1: Value contributions of IT in enterprises

The use of IT is often initiated by single departments in a company, for example when the front office implements a payment system or the back office a billing application. With their first online presence the reach of their offer increases and helps to address customers outside of the own region.

As soon as entire departments use IT, value contributions increase significantly. The model in figure 2 shows departments suitable for IT support. In many cases standard software for the offer and order management, billing and accounting is the initial equipment. Later, CRM systems (Customer Relationship Management) for marketing and sales are added. CAM applications (Computer-aided Manufacturing) support production control, other software the automated voucherless commissioning. Management information systems (MIS) provide key performance indicators (KPIs) from planning, controlling and quality assurance to supporting the management. Using IT makes cost savings and hence an increased productivity possible. As a consequence, the price of products can be used as a competitive advantage.

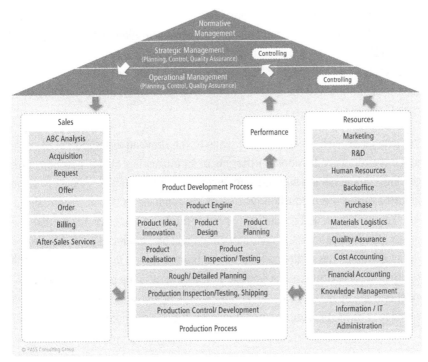

Figure 2: Reference model for enterprises

At the next stage, internal IT systems were integrated with each other (EAI, Enterprise Application Integration). This leads to the elimination of media breaks and the automation of business processes. This is often followed by the integration of suppliers into their own processes (SCM/Supply Chain Management and eProcurement). This way, the enterprise achieves transparency of alternative supplier offers and can manage its purchasing in order to get deliveries exactly when they are needed by the production process. This reduces lead times and the costs for own stock-keeping. High availability and short delivery times of the own products create additional competitive advantages.

The next important step is the use of the internet for presenting own products and for direct orders. But the global presence of an own virtual shop does not only expand the customer base. It also increases the number of suppliers who are comparable and in direct competition. Here, the integration of payment systems and logistic providers is a chance to develop delivery time as a new competitive advantage. Other options for differentiation are the attractiveness of the products, their presentation and the usability of the web shop. All of this requires appropriate IT solutions.

In many cases such a development leads to the growing virtualization of more and more company divisions. Purchasing, order processing, billing, payments processing, commissioning and shipping only require interacting IT systems. In some industries even the production process or the products itself can be virtualized. An example of this is bookselling, where seconds after a customer's order the payment will be processed, a (virtual) eBook will be "produced" and transferred to the eBook reader of the customer or its representation in the cloud. Even the return process is virtualized: a credit note will be sent to the payment service provider and the book will be deleted on the eBook reader. A company working that way does not waste resources, and it pollutes the environment only by the power consumption of the involved IT systems. It is able to react quickly to changes of the value chain, for example to competitor's offers with more attractive supplementary services, new markets, a fluctuation in demand, and so on. Actually virtualized enterprises still need employees, but with skills which are complementary to the machines in use: They must use their creativity for innovations t o enable their company to stand out from the competition.

This development neither comes overnight nor does it have the same speed in all industries. The following chapter gives an overview of the emerging use of IT in particular industries and for each decade since 1960.

# The use of information technology from 1960 to 2015

### 1960 to 1969

In the 60s the use of IT is rather an exception. In commerce, larger companies use computers for inventory management and accounting. To make this possible also for smaller companies, DATEV is founded in 1966. Its mission is to provide bookkeeping services for business clients on the basis of IT.

Banks and insurance companies operate own mainframes. Data is primarily processed by batch jobs - without user interactions.

Computer-aided manufacturing (CAM) finds its way into the industrial production.

The first digital networks start a new era of communication, for example the Arpanet, which is regarded as the precursor of the internet.

## 1970 to 1979

In the early 70s credit agencies use IT to collect information about individuals and to offer electronic inquiry services regarding their credit standing.

The SWIFT network paves the way for electronic messaging and for transactions between banks, brokerage houses, stock exchanges and other financial institutions. Banks implement the voucherless data carrier exchange for bank transfers and direct debiting. Insurance companies use IT for their risk management.

In the travel industry IT enables the creation of new companies with new business models. They collate data in large data centers and offer travel agents access to their computerized reservation systems (CRS) by simple, character-based terminals for the query of prices, availability information and for bookings.

First mainframe-based systems for production control are used in industrial production. In cars IT is coming up in the form of on-board computers. In the USA, Compuserve is founded as the first commercial online service provider which offers for example electronic mail exchange services for the users of the first emerging personal computers (PCs).

## 1980 to 1989

In the 80s personal computers con-
quer the market and open IT for the
mass market. Thus, cashless payment
by means of magnetic cards becomes available for retail enterprises
and PC-based electronic point-of-
sale (EPOS) systems for the overall
commerce.

Especially communication is making
good progress. In the USA, CompuServe allows for the first real-time chats. In
Germany the roll-out of an early video text system called "Bildschirmtext" starts
in 1980, and the digital communication network ISDN (Integrated Services Digital
Network) becomes implemented nationwide by the end of the 80s.

Driven by this progress in electronic communication, the first direct insurers emerge where insurance policies can be contracted online. They compete with the
mostly cumbersome processes and sales organizations of large insurance groups.

The travel industry is characterized by a growing interconnection, where new ge-
nerations of computerized reservation systems (CRS) now enable travel agencies
to trade tickets of different airlines.

In logistics, innovations also take place in the 80s. New supply chain management
(SCM) systems allow the integration of planning, optimization and controlling
processes and the tracking of material, information and financial flows from the
first supplier up to the final consumer. There are first approaches for the automated voucherless commissioning supported by robots.

In Germany public administrations are using IT widely with great restraint, while Austria launches its e-government portal help.gv.at and a citizen card function among other things for electronic identification. Germany develops an electronic dunning process which is still based on the exchange of storage media.

In automobiles, IT allows for more and more assistance systems such as the anti-lock braking system, dynamics and stability controls, a brake assistant, a tire pressure control system, adaptive cruise control and lane assistant, a high-beam assistant, and so on.

In the entertainment industry, MP3 is established as a standard for saving and transferring music on computers and on portable music players. The first movies are created where large parts are computer-generated.

## 1990 to 1999

The 1990s are dominated by the internet. CompuServe with more than 10 years of experience in the USA becomes the first mass provider of internet access in Germany. Even mobile communication becomes digital. GSM becomes the standard for fully digital mobile phone networks  such as D1, which was introduced in Germany in 1992. In the same year, IBM launches the first smartphone in the USA, which can send e-mails and faxes, manage a calendar and an address book and allows gaming. The miniaturization and the development of the bandwidth enables more and more users to dispatch e-mails, keep chats and use internet-based applications on their mobile devices. The decade ends with the launch of the first camera phone.

The internet enables the financial industry to a seamless automation of its processes. Straight through processing (STP) allows the same-day processing of money market and security transactions.

In the 90s, the travel industry undergoes a very impressive development. In 1990 travel sales become independent of specific computerized reservation systems (CRS). Integrated solutions allow for availability and price requests to multiple reservation systems at the same time and for selecting a matching response based on the customer's criteria (or those of the travel agency). This transparency optimizes the travel sales business where CRSs now face an aggressive competition. Finally, in 1997, internet booking engines (IBE) allow the traveler direct enquiring and booking – in addition to flights also for hotels, rental cars, rail connections, and so on. Due to the internet, the travelers can now directly compare for example the offers of travel agencies or airlines directly.

Even manufacturing companies are being penetrated by IT more and more. In 1990, the first PC-based production planning and control systems are available. With SAP R/2 the first standard system for enterprise resource planning (ERP) enters the market.

The progress in digital mobile communication helps the logistics industry to optimize their processes by mobile data capturing. IT allows the implementation of concepts such as demand management (pull approach), on-time respectively just-in-time delivery and the minimization of stock keeping.

In Germany, the first public authorities start to provide forms and documents with an own presence in the internet in 1990. In 1999, the German tax authority launches ELSTER, a system for the electronic creation and transmission of income-tax declarations. Austria introduces the electronic legal communication of requests to regional courts.

Cars use GPS-based navigation systems with integrated congestion information and dynamic route guidance.

In 1990, the entertainment industry launches the first game consoles with 3D graphics capability and internet access. The first internet-based music file-sharing platform is founded. The standard MPEG-4 allows video telephony, video digitalization and video usage even with few resources or small bandwidths.

## 2000 to 2009

In the first years of the new millennium the industry-wide IT penetration continues, supported by the expansion of the global communications infrastructure, especially high-speed internet access and the increased geographical coverage of mobile broadband even in rural regions.

Smartphones get own operating systems: first Apple's iPhone, followed by devices with Android one year later. This enables the development of applications which can run directly on mobile devices and can operate independently of location and distance to any server.

Virtual credit accounts are a big boost for online commerce: Customers pay into accounts managed by companies such as PayPal or ClickAndBuy, which are available for online shopping. Virtual marketplaces make it easier for prospective buyers to search and compare different offers regarding price, product or service characteristics, customer  reviews and other aspects. As a result, all suppliers are faced with a national, even global competition with highest transparency for the customers.

In banks, the increasing automation reaches complex decision-making processes. Customers can enter a credit application in the internet, which passes through a complex set of rules and, in case of a positive rating, will be completed automatically. In 2000, the first direct banks emerge in Germany: banks without a branch network of their own, which perform their business completely via the internet. Appropriate software for smartphones allows mobile banking, making bank customers not only independent of bank branches but also of stationary computers and their internet access point at home.

Insurance companies also use IT to automate complex decision-making processes. Consumers can request an offer for a life insurance from various vendors via the internet and conclude it with their prefered provider.

In logistics, route planning systems automatically assign vehicles to orders, based on mathematical models and algorithms. For each vehicle this software finds the optimal sequential order of the destinations with regard to either time or costs.

In the first decade of the new millennium, most of the public administrations are available on the internet supporting different affairs of the citizens. German citizens can now use an online portal to submit their tax declaration.

Even the German judicial system uses IT more and more. The electronic court and administration inbox enables courts in Germany to exchange information securely and legally binding. Germany also launches its electronic commercial and company register.

The entertainment industry offers video on demand services, where consumers have access to almost any movie which is available in digital form. Gaming consoles with extended online functionality allow playing together via the internet, motion control, and so on. With Second Life users can slip into the shape of an avatar and interact, play or even trade in virtual worlds.

## 2010 bis 2019

The trend towards global competition continues. Shops available in the internet do not only compare prices, product characteristics or delivery times of different suppliers but also customer reviews and personal recommendations. They refer to related information in social networks and show what other buyers of a specific product have viewed or bought.

In the production industry, first model factories of a Smart Factory arise. Components inform the machines about how they must be handled. Machines and plants

exchange data in real-time, interact with each other and optimize themselves. The German Federal Government supports this development, calling it "Industry 4.0". Its objective is a highly flexible industrial mass production of highly individualized products. At the same time, however, another innovation enters the market which jeopardizes this objective of the industrial production: 3D printers allow the production of simple products directly by the consumer.

The progresses of IT at public administrations are less futuristic. The German Federal Government adopts the eGovernment Act which obliges all authorities at federal, state and municipal levels to be electronically accessible. It regulates the electronic keeping and handling of files and simplifies electronic payments in administrative procedures. First approaches of electronic files are also evident in judiciary. Other countries launch electronic voting.

In the years beyond 2010 even vehicles are connected to the internet more and more. This enables the communication between vehicles and with the surrounding infrastructure. Advanced IT-based assistance systems increase the safety of vehicles because they can automatically detect pedestrians, correct driving errors or register micro-sleep. They foresee accident risks and automatically brake and bring a vehicle to a halt if, for example, there is a risk of a rear-end collision. IT enables self-steering cars (at least some prototypes) to drive through the traffic of a large city.

## What could the future look like?

In 1926 the soviet economist Nikolai Kondratiev published his theory of long economic cycles, the so called "Kondratiev Waves" [Korotayev/Tsirel 2010]. He described the ups and downs of the economy in waves of 50 to 60 years. Each upswing is accompanied by a new basic innovation, in which investments are made until the turning point has been reached. This is almost a disruptive innovation, which helps the economy to record a spurt in growth by eliminating restrictions. One example is the invention of the railroad together with a transnational rail network, which improved the delivery of raw materials and the distribution of industrially manufactured products, which had been transported by horse-drawn carts on country roads until then.

About 25 years later, such a basic innovation is generally accepted, established and an integral part of daily life. Over time new restrictions arise which lead to another downswing. Investments in this technology are dwindling. During this downswing new developments pave the way for the next basic innovation.

The previous chapter showed how the internet initiates the upswing of the 5th Kondratiev wave in the middle of the 1990s. The expression internet stands for the integration of all partners along the value chain such as suppliers, customers, payment and logistics service providers, as well as the possibility of global marketing and the resulting entry into a global innovation and time-based competition.

According to Kondratiev this upswing will continue until about 2020. Then investments in the use of the internet will decrease. In the following 25 years investments will be made in the next important basic innovation, which will probably initiate the upswing of another Kondratiev wave. It can be anticipated that thereby other restrictions of our daily live will be eliminated - supported by IT. Some approaches and trends of today already indicate which restrictions will be affected.

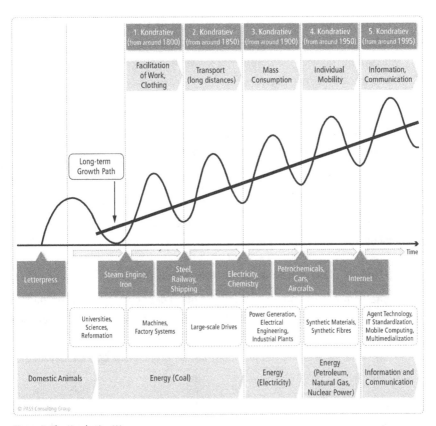

Figure 3: The Kondratiev Waves

## • **We get rid of limitations by local constraint**

Smart Learning makes learning independent of time and place. Especially people in regions without access to educational institutions can come together in virtual classrooms with other learners and teachers from all over the world. Access to knowledge is no longer a privilege of industrial nations.

Enterprises no longer have to depend on employees, who not only have the required skills, but also live close to the planned place of work or have the according mobility. Cooperation in a team now only requires internet access and a common language.

The distribution of industrially manufactured products becomes superfluous because the production will be performed by a 3D printer close to the consumer – or directly by the consumer's own 3D printer.

Smart Travel allows visiting popular destinations without itineraries, travel costs, waiting queues, and so on. Today Google Street View can already be used for Smart Travel. In the near future the experience will be more realistic by using virtual reality glasses.

- **„Things" become smart and relieve people**

Smart materials inform the production machines how they must be handled. After production has been finished, a process of predictive maintenance starts: Smart components monitor the operability of the product and report any need for repair or replacement before it comes to operational restrictions.

In the "Internet of Things" smart equipment enriched with IT, also called cyber-physical systems (CPS), communicate with each other. Already today some vehicles exchange information with each other and with the transport infrastructure to find a route and speed which are optimal at the given moment, or to reduce the risks of accidents. When this becomes standard on our roads traffic lights, regulations and traffic signs may no longer be necessary.

Robots take over more and more tasks and thereby relieve people. Today industrial robots, household robots such as robotic lawn-mowers or independently operating robotic vacuum cleaners, robots for bomb-disposal or other dangerous missions are the most popular ones. With suitable programming robots even compete against each other in football matches.

- **We get rid of limitations by matter and by the laws of physics: „Things" become virtual**

Most smartphone users carry these "things" with them permanently: pocket calculator, address book, notepad, dictaphone, music player, camera, watch, compass, spirit level, pocket lamp, calendar, different dictionaries

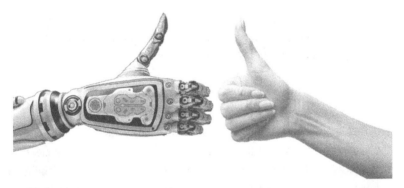

and city maps, a library of own books, and so on. Not the real objects, of course, but apps, virtualized objects, their functionality nevertheless equal to the real ones.

Virtual reality glasses allow for a realistic experience of artificial locations, buildings, facilities, game worlds, and so on, that are non-existent in the real world.

- **We get rid of limitations by human physicality and the human organism**

  Already today, IT controlled implants can help with some diseases and physical decline. Some implants of chips such as brain pacemakers for Patients with Parkinson's Disease have been successful. Research is working to understand forgetfulness and seeks a solution for retrierving memories.

  Japan, the most quickly ageing country, shows the world how the crisis in the health care sector can be solved by robotic nurses. These machines distribute medicines in hospitals, transport their human patients, move and wash them and shampoo their hair.

  When meeting other people in virtual conference rooms or game worlds we can – regardless of our appearance or physical disabilities in the real world – select an avatar to represent ourselves.

## The importance of productive software development

Whether the economy follows Nikolai Kondratiev's waves or not, one look at the evolution of IT and at the emerging trends of the near future clearly shows that success will depend more and more on the short-term availability of new software-based innovations. Thus, the IT industry plays a key role. Issues such as the calculability of IT projects, productivity of software development processes and software quality become critical success factors. In this context important tasks for software developing companies are standardization and re-use, automation of development and quality assurance processes as well as measurements of the performance and product quality. In particular, regular measurements of the productivity are crucial for planning delivery milestones reliably and control the effectiveness of improvement measures.

# III. What is Productivity and how can it be measured?

The previous chapter clearly showed the importance of software development for the economic upswing. Often only IT-based innovations enable enterprises to stand out from the competition. This increases the time pressure on software developing companies and requires reliable planning methods.

The next chapters will show that regular measurements of the productivity are crucial to plan the development effort and delivery milestones reliably. In this context, estimates are unsuitable. First, this chapter will clarify what productivity is and which aspects of productivity are relevant for software development processes.

## Different aspects of productivity

From the view of an entire company and considering production, marketing, sales and human resources, the following aspects of productivity can be distinguished [Grönroos/Ojasalo 2002]:

- **Efficiency**, which is an internal aspect and considers the profitability of production regarding a cost / benefit relation:

$$\text{Efficiency} = \frac{\text{Production Outcome}}{\text{Expense}}$$

    When considering software development as a production process, the production outcome corresponds to the output of produced software, and the expense equals the work performance.

- **Capacity**, which is affected by both the ability to flexibly react to changes in demand and also by optimizing the workload of the staff.

- **Effectiveness** as the ratio between the objective achieved and the intended objective. It is derived from price determining external factors such as the market position, image, the valuation of the product or service quality by customers, the quality of interaction with customers, and so on.

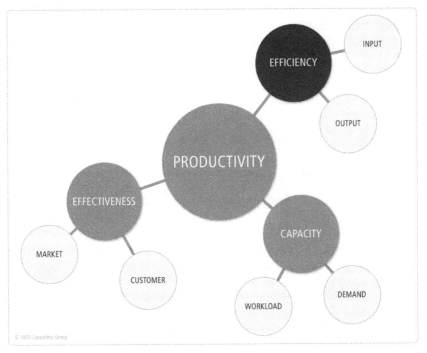

Figure 4: Productivity from a business point of view

## Productivity of software development

In order to achieve a reliable estimation of the development effort, it is sufficient to focus on the (internal) production process. In this case, price determining external factors can be disregarded. Furthermore, the disposition and workload of employees is of subordinate importance when considering particular development projects. Thus measuring productivity can be reduced to the efficiency or rather the profitability of the production process:

$$\text{Productivity} \ = \ \frac{\text{Output}}{\text{Input}}$$

In this case output is the size of the produced software and input the effort for personnel expenses:

$$\text{Productivity} \ = \ \frac{\text{Size}}{\text{Effort}}$$

The following chapters describe the four necessary requirements which must be fulfilled before an organisation can measure the productivity of its software development processes.

## Requirement 1: Process scope is defined consistently

Productivity is a process metric. Therefore it requires a determination and boundary of the process to be considered for the measurement. It is recommended to determine the process scope as wide as possible to have all activities and phases of the project included. The measurement of particular project tasks such as the requirements analysis, conception, implementation, functional testing, and so on requires a precise separation of these phases, which means a precise determination of each beginning and end. In today's practice of software development, which is often iterative or incremental, phases are no longer separated as it was typical for the waterfall model. Thus, it is better to measure complete processes instead of tasks or phases in order to use these measurements for cost estimations of complete processes as well.

The comparability of productivity values of development processes measured with different approaches, tools or paradigms (e. g. model-driven software development, traditional programming, customizing of standard systems, and so on) also requires measuring the entire process. A proven process scope ranges from the start of the conceptualization to production handover. Only if beginning and end of the measured processes are the same, the comparison of the measured productivity values is suitable for evaluating which approaches or paradigms are more efficient.

## Requirement 2: Final product quality is consistent

In addition to the definition of the process scope, it is important that all considered processes finish with a consistent quality. This can be ensured by a final quality gate at the end of the process, which defines common quality criteria for the produced software. Otherwise neglecting quality assurance results in reduced costs and thus (for this process) in an apparently increased productivity. However, the impact on the next increments and on further developments are additional costs due to defect analyses and bugfixings. In other words: QA costs saved during the initial new development add to the further development costs.

## Requirement 3: Input is measurable

The input value of productivity measurement, this means the effort, results from the total work performance of all employees involved in the process, calculated in man days. Productivity measurements can only work if this total work performance can be determined accurately and reliably. It must be ensured that the measurement does not include working time of the employees they did not dedicate to the considered project. Moreover, the working time of those employees must be included, who do not belong to the project team but support it to a small extent.

Working time where a project has been supported but which is not included in the input value for the measurement makes productivity seem better than it really is. In contrast, working hours where the employee has not supported the project but which have been allocated to the project because of comfort or due to the inadequacy of the booking system result in a seemingly worse productivity.

## Requirement 4: Output is measurable

The greatest challenge is quantifying the output of a software development process. This requires a metric for measuring the size of the software. In the next chapter, requirements for such size metrics will be described and related standards and sample methods along with their pros and cons will be shown: A pro can be the low measurement effort for automizing measurements, a con the need for assessing in stead of counting.

Determining the expected expenses of planned development activities requires a large number of empirical values. Thus, it is not enough to launch the most popular measuring method. It must be applied consistantly over a longer period. Any change of the method leads to an interruption of the empirical measurements and the impact is that measurements before and after the interruption cannot be compared with each other.

# IV. Methods for measuring the Development Output

## Requirements on a size metric

When planning to introduce regular productivity measurement, the first challenge is the choice of a suitable measuring method. The reliability of determined expected expenses of planned development activities as well as the transparency of the effectiveness of improvement measures, depend on the quality of this method to a large extent.

The following three scientific criteria for the assessment of measuring methods give a first orientation:

- **Objectivity**: The measured values shall be independent of the measuring person. It is not acceptable that different persons applying the same method to the same measuring object come up with different results. However, this is the consequence when methods use pure estimations and criteria are not sharply defined. Instead, methods shall count objects according to precise rules.

- **Reliability** (also: Reproducibility): Repeated measurements shall reach the same results. It is not acceptable that repeated measurements of the same measuring object applying the same method come up with different results. This is further effect of rules that are not sharply defined and hence can be interpreted differently.

- **Validity**: Measured values must represent the variable to be measured. There must be a clear correlation between the measured values and the characteristics of the measured object which is to be measured. Size itself is an abstract expression; the targeted characteristics must be determined precisely, for example, by counting the lines of a program or the number of status transitions.

These quality factors build upon each other: validity requires reliability and objectivity.

In addition to these scientific criteria, there are the following practical requirements for methods measuring software size:

- Independency of technological aspects. The influence of technological aspects on productivity can only become transparent if the applied measuring method is independent. Only then, the improvements by using, for example, a different development paradigm, a framework or changes of the architecture can be quantified. Even the programming language or coding style should not affect the measured values: Projects relying on service orientation and re-use which produce fewer code are, hence, not less productive than others which copy long code structures for similar program flows and tend to a complicated programming style.

- Measurements must be possible before and after the implementation of software as well. In practice, measuring the size of an existing application is as important as determining it, based on a business concept or functional specification, before the implementation starts. A method which counts code lines is not feasible for pre-implementation measurements.

- Economy, ability of automation. There must be a reasonable relationship between the measuring effort and the total effort of the project. Since size measurements must be performed multiple times during the development process, a method is preferable which can run fully or partly automatic. The initial effort for implementing related scripts or programs is not unimportant. But at each subsequent measurement, for example, when a new increment or release is completed, the measuring effort is reduced to calling such scripts or programs.

## Code metrics

Line-of-code (LOC) metrics have been the first approach for measuring the development size. They are as old as programming itself. These metrics are based on counting source code lines and measure the length of a program. There are different versions, which can be distinguished by the types of code lines to be counted:

- Source lines of code without empty and comment lines (SLOC).

- Only comment lines of code (CLOC). In quality management this metric is helpful for the quantitative valuation of the code's commentation such as comment density, which is the quotient of the number of comment lines (CLOC) and the total number of code lines (LOC).

- The number of statements (NOS), also called number of logical lines of code (LLOC). This variant counts statements independent from their distribution among various code lines. Therefore the influence of the coding style is limited.

One problem of using code metrics for measuring the output of a software development process is that the number of code lines or statements does not correlate with the requirements that have been implemented. Using such output measurements for determining the productivity will have the effect that those projects seem to be more productive which are characterised by a bad coding style, complicate programming and which produce a lot of redundant code. Actually projects based on encapsulating and re-using frequently used functionality are more productive. Another disadvantage of code metrics is that measured values in different programming languages are not comparable.

Code metrics can be useful in some areas of quality management, for example, for weighting values as in the case of comment density. Measuring is simple and can be automated easily. However, these metrics are not suitable for determining productivity of a software development process.

## Functional size measurement

To prevent problems from arising when using code metrics, the term of functional size has been coined already in the 80s and used 1997 to define the standard ISO/IEC 14143 [ISO/IEC 14143 2007]. Functional size measurement (FSM) considers the functional requirements (also called functional user requirements, FURs) and disregards non-functional requirements (NFURs). From today's perspective it is a proven practice to separate FURs from NFURs: In modern software development most non-functional requirements can be met by architecture and/or design standards, whereas functional requirements (depending on the degree of individuality) are often subject of development processes, where measurement methods are needed for effort estimations and productivity measurements. This does not mean that NFURs can be generally ignored, but they must be considered in a different way than FURs, which will be described in detail in the context of effort estimations in the second book of this series.

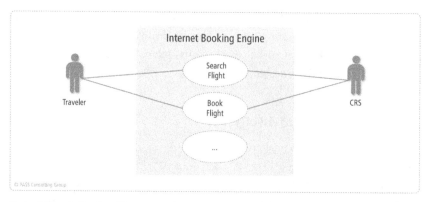

Figure 5: Sample Use Case Diagram

Functional requirements can be derived from use cases of a system. A use case re-presents the behavior of the system which can be perceived by an actor from out-side (related to the defined sytem boundaries), who interacts with it. Actors can be human users as well as external systems or machines (any pieces of hardware or software). Figure 5 shows an example: the use case diagram of a (simplified) internet booking engine for flights. Within the system boundaries (represented by the rectangle with the label „Internet Booking Engine") use cases are represented by ellipses. They are used by actors, in the example a traveler and a computerized reservation system (CRS), which is indicated by lines from the actors to the use cases.

| Use Case: | Search Flight |
|---|---|
| Primary Actor: | Traveler |
| Precondition: | Traveler opened the Flight Search dialog |
| Basic Flow: | 1) Traveler enters flight date |
| | 2) Traveler enters first letters of the destination (name or code) |
| | 3) System checks database table for matching airports and displays a list showing names and airport codes |
| | 4) Traveler selects an entry of the list and clicks the ‚Search" button |
| | 5) System sends a „Flight Search Request" message to the CRS including date and airport code |
| | 6) System receives a „Flight Search Response" message from the CRS and reads fields „departure time, arrival time, airline name, flight number, class, price, currency code" of all included flight records |
| | 7) System displays all flight records showing these fields in a dialog table |

Table 1: Sample BFCs of a Use Case

Each use case consists of multiple actions performing the particular functionality, which are called „Base Functional Components" (BFCs). Table 1 shows the (simplified) BFCs as the basic flow of use case „Search Flight". BFCs are the basis for functional size measurement, which therefore can be done before the implementation of software has been started – as soon as the FURs are known. Thus, the functional size is independent of the source code or any technical characteristics and therefore better suited for valid measurements of the output of a software development process, which is one of the main requirements for measuring productivity.

## Function Point Analysis

Driven by the problems with code metrics, Allan J. Albrecht developed the Function Point Analysis (FPA, also: Function Points Method) at the end of the 70s. It is based on the analysis of use cases, where elementary processes[1] (input, output or queries across system boundaries) and related data structures can be derived from.

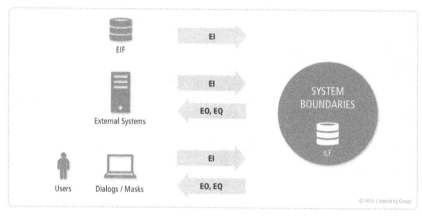

Figure 6: Objects to be counted by the Function Point Analysis

For performing a Function Point Analysis, a definition of the system boundaries, this means a differentiation which use cases or sub-systems are within the scope of size measurement and which are not, is required first. After this, the following objects have to be counted:

- Elementary processes, where actors of use cases (users as well as external systems) process data of the system. Here, the following transactional functions have to be considered:

---

1  These represent the Base Functional Components (BFCs) as described by the standard ISO/IEC 14143 for Functional Size Measurement. "Elementary" means, that these processes cannot be further divided into sub processes with own interactions.

- External Input (EI): Data coming from outside crosses the system boundaries - within the scope of a use case.
- External Output (EO): Data crosses the system boundaries to the outside – within the scope of a use case.
- External Inquiry (EQ): Because data also crosses the boundaries to the outside and with regard to automated counting, inquiries are often handled as output.

- Data structures in the database which represent business objects and which are relevant for the elementary processes described before. Depending on the storage location, whether within or outside of the system boundaries, the following types are distinguished:

  - Internal Logical File (ILF): Data structure, where the data is maintained by the system itself. This means insert, delete and update functionalities are use cases of the considered system.
  - External Interface File (EIF): Data structure, where the system performs read-only access. This means insert, delete and update functionalities are no use cases of the considered system

When counting these objects, their weights follow rules which are oriented towards their complexity:

- The weight of an elementary process (EI, EO or EQ) depends on the number of different data fields involved (also called Data Element Types, DETs) and the number of different files involved (also called File Types Referenced, FTRs). It is determined by open-ended, three-leveled interval scales:

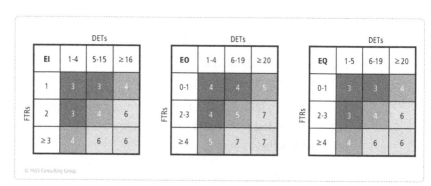

Figure 7: Weighting matrices for elementary processes

- The weight of a data structure (ILF or EIF) depends on the number of different data fields involved (also called Data Element Types, DETs) and the number of different field groups involved (also called Record Element Types, RETs). A field group is a cluster of associated fields, for example the name of a person, which consists of title, first and last name or the postal address, which in the simplest case is a combination of street, street number, zip code and city. Hence, a personal address is an ILF built by the two field groups (RETs) name and postal address with 7 fields (DETs) in total. Here too, the weights are determined by open-ended, three-leveled interval scales:

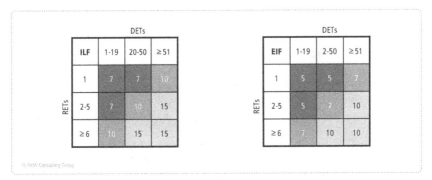

Figure 8: Weighting matrices for data structures

Finally, the functional size of the measured software results in the sum of all weights of elementary processes and related data structures. In many cases counting can be automized, as described by the Object Management Group [OMG/FP 2013].

Table 2 shows the functional size of sample use case „Search Flight" determined by using the Function Point Analysis.

Use Case:         Search Flight
Primary Actor:    Traveler
Precondition:     Traveler opened the Flight Search dialog

1) Traveler enters flight date
2) Traveler enters first letters of the destination (name or code)

EI with 1 FTR and 2 DETs (date value and sub-string of destination name or code)       1 EI x 3 = **3**

3) System checks database table for matching airports and displays a list showing names and airport codes

EIF with 1 RET and 2 DETs       1 EIF x 5 = **5**

4) Traveler selects an entry of the list and clicks the „Search" button

EI with 1 FTR and 1 DET (ID of the selected list entry)       1 EI x 3 = **3**

5) System sends a „Flight Search Request" message to the CRS including date and airport code

EO with 1 FTR and 2 DETs (XML file including date value and airport code)       1 EO x 4 = **4**

6) System receives a „Flight Search Response" message from the CRS and reads fields „departure time, arrival time, airline name, flight number, class, price, currency code" of all included flight records

EI with 1 FTR and 7 DETs (XML file including departure time, arrival time, airline name, flight number, class, price and currency code)       1 EI x 3 = **3**

7) System displays all flight records showing these fields in a dialog table

EO with 1 FTR and 7 DETs (dialog table with columns „departure time, arrival time, airline name, flight number, class, price and currency code")       1 EO x 4 = **4**

---

**Functional size = 22 FP**

---

Table 2: Functional Size of Sample Use Case „Search Flight" measured by FPA

In practice, the approximation method Rapid is widely used. It generally assumes the medium weight for elementary processes (4 for EIs and 5 for EOs) and the lowest weight for data structures (7 for ILFs and 5 for ELFs). This reduces the effort for counting, but the influence of complexity is being considered even less and the inaccuracy increases.

The version of the Function Point Analysis described in this chapter has been standardised by the International Function Point Users Group (IFPUG) as ISO/IEC 20926 [ISO/IEC 20926 2009]. Some variants have also been standardised, such as the Mark II FPA method by the UKSMA (United Kingdom Software Metrics Association) or the methods of the FISMA (Finnish Software Measurement Association) and the NESMA (Netherlands Software Metrics users Association). However the method of IFPUG is the most popular in the world. In many software developing companies it is the best known method for functional measurement.

## The COSMIC Method

It is obvious that you improve the accuracy of measurements by directly counting the involved data elements instead of the elementary processes and data structures. In the 80s this approach lead to the development of the so called Full Function Points (FFP) method. Based on this, the Common Software Measurement International Consortium [COSMIC 2015] was founded in 1998. Five year later, the FFP or COSMIC method has been accepted as the new standard ISO/IEC 19761 [COSMIC FSM 2014].

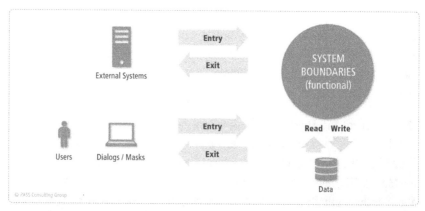

Figure 9: Objects to be counted by the COSMIC Method

COSMIC follows the standard ISO/IEC 14143 for functional size measurement and considers basic functional components (elementary[2] functional processes of the use cases). It uses an extended definition of actors, the so-called functional users, which, in addition to human users and external systems, include various pieces of hardware or software such as input or output devices, which can send and receive data across the system boundaries and trigger functional processes of the considered system. Independent of the type of functional users, COSMIC counts all use case related and disjoint data elements per elementary functional process which cross the system boundaries and/or are stored into or retrieved from the database. COSMIC calls these objects data movements and distinguishes the following types:

- Entry: One or more data elements used by a functional process are cross the system boundaries from the direction of an actor.

---

2 "Elementary" means, that these processes cannot be divided further into sub processes with own interactions.

- Exit: One or more data elements used by a functional process cross the system boundaries towards an actor.

- Read: One or more data elements are read from a persistent memory and used by a functional process.

- Write: One or more data elements from a functional process are stored in a persistent memory.

This way, data operations, transformations, enrichments, and so on, are not relevant for counting. In contrast to the Function Point Analysis, COSMIC considers read and write operations of different data elements instead of the static size of data structures. Finally the functional size of a measured system is the number of

| Use Case: | Search Flight |
|---|---|
| Primary Actor: | Traveler |
| Precondition: | Traveler opened the Flight Search dialog |

| | |
|---|---:|
| 1) Traveler enters flight date | |
| date value | **1** Entry |
| 2) Traveler enters first letters of the destination (name or code) | |
| sub-string of destination name or code | **1** Entry |
| 3) System checks database table for matching airports and displays a list showing names and airport codes | |
| reference table with 2 attributes | **2** Read |
| 4) Traveler selects an entry of the list and clicks the „Search" button | |
| ID of the selected list entry | **1** Entry |
| 5) System sends a „Flight Search Request" message to the CRS including date and airport code | |
| XML file including date value and airport code | **2** Exit |
| 6) System receives a „Flight Search Response" message from the CRS and reads fields „departure time, arrival time, airline name, flight number, class, price, currency code" of all included flight records | |
| XML file including departure time, arrival time, airline name, flight number, class, price and currency code | **7** Entry |
| 7) System displays all flight records showing these fields in a dialog table | |
| dialog table with columns „departure time, arrival time, airline name, flight number, class, price and currency code" | **7** Exit |

**Functional size = 21 FFP**

Table 3: Functional Size of Sample Use Case „Search Flight" measured by COSMIC

all data movements. Table 3 shows the functional size of sample use case „Search Flight" determined by using the COSMIC method.

The COSMIC method does not consider the complexity of the functional processes. Originally, it does not differentiate weights of the counted objects, this means, all data elements have the same score whether they are read or written, entered on a dialog or just displayed on a report. This is useful and simplifies measurement if data validation and preparation for input and output is characterized by similar complexity, for example, in case of transactional or real-time systems. However, it is typical for most business applications that the input of data represents a higher functional size than the output for read only purposes, due to the required checks regarding value range, consistency, and so on. Moreover, the functional size represented by storing data in a database consistently, is higher than by reading data.

## The Data Interaction Point Method

Looking for a method which counts objects with the granularity of data elements by not requiring any estimation and which is suitable for measuring even large business applications, PASS Consulting Group developed the Data Interaction Point (DIP) method in 2006 [PASS 2013]. According to the standard ISO/IEC 14143 it focuses on use cases. The method considers data elements crossing the system boundaries and interacting with actors (human users, external systems or devices) as well as the databases where these data elements are stored. Contrary to the Function Point Analysis, no elementary processes were counted apart from the involved data elements, and no data structures apart from the elements they comprise:

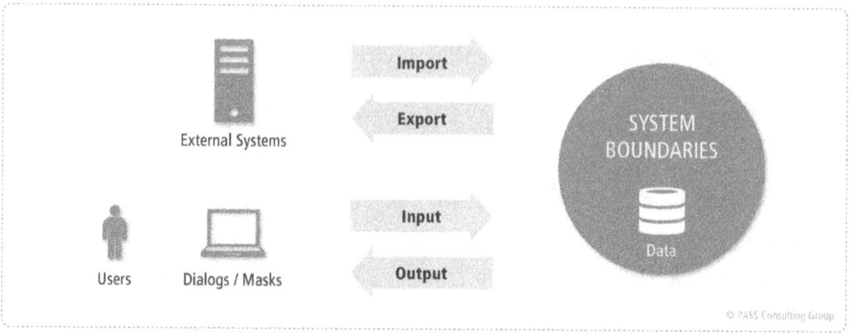

Figure 10: Objects to be counted by the Data Interaction Point Method

- Database: The method counts the number of different data elements which are involved in use cases.

- User interface: Objects to be counted are all data elements which can be entered or displayed on dialogs or masks within the scope of use cases.

- Interfaces to external systems or devices, that is, import or export functions: Here the method considers all data elements crossing the system boundaries to be processed or displayed in one of the related systems.

Similar to the Function Point Analysis, the weights of the objects to be counted correlate with the complexity of pre- and post-processing. The DIP method derives these weights from the usage of a data element, for example, depending on whether a data element enters the system via a dialog or an interface, where value and consistency checks are required, or is simply displayed or put out without pre-processing. Weights can be varied, depending on system types such as business or transactional/real-time applications. The following weights have proved their worth for applications with a strong focus on user interactions and dialogs:

- Dialogs/ masks: Value 3 for elements which can be entered by an actor (type: UI-I), 1 for elements which are only displayed (type: UI-O).
- Database: Value 3 for elements which can be changed by the considered system (type: DB), 1 for elements which are only read (type: REF).
- Interfaces/ imports/ exports: Values between 1 and 2 depending on the input/ output validations (types: IMP, EXP).

Table 4 shows the functional size of the sample use case „Search Flight" determined by using the Data Interaction Point method.

| Use Case: | Search Flight |
|---|---|
| Primary Actor: | Traveler |
| Precondition: | Traveler opened the Flight Search dialog |

| | |
|---|---:|
| 1) Traveler enters flight date | |
| date value | 1 UI-I x 3 = **3** |
| 2) Traveler enters first letters of the destination (name or code) | |
| sub-string of destination name or code | 1 UI-I x 3 = **3** |
| 3) System checks database table for matching airports and displays a list showing names and airport codes | |
| reference table with 2 attributes | 2 REF x 1 = **2** |
| 4) Traveler selects an entry of the list and clicks the „Search" button | |
| ID of the selected list entry | 1 UI-I x 3 = **3** |
| 5) System sends a „Flight Search Request" message to the CRS including date and airport code | |
| XML file including date value and airport code | 2 EXP x 1 = **2** |
| 6) System receives a „Flight Search Response" message from the CRS and reads fields „departure time, arrival time, airline name, flight number, class, price, currency code" of all included flight records | |
| XML file including departure time, arrival time, airline name, flight number, class, price and currency code | 7 IMP x 1 = **7** |
| 7) System displays all flight records showing these fields in a dialog table | |
| dialog table with columns „departure time, arrival time, airline name, flight number, class, price and currency code" | 7 UI-O x 1 = **7** |

**Functional size = 27 DIP**

Table 4: Functional Size of Sample Use Case „Search Flight" measured by DIP

Due to the relatively straightforward determination of the weights, measurement with the DIP method can usually be performed with less effort than, for example, with the Function Point Analysis. Moreover, counting can be automated easily because the data elements to be counted can mostly be derived from structural characteristics such as code pattern, database metadata, models, XML schemes, and so on.

## Comparison of measurement methods

Figure 11 shows the results of measurements of different systems performed with the three functional size metrics described previously [3] [4]:

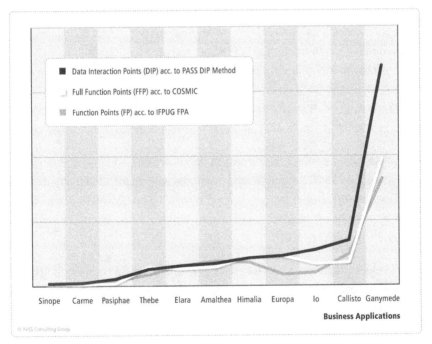

Figure 11: Comparison of size measurements of different systems by FPA, COSMIC and DIP

---

3   Source: Field study of the PASS Consulting Group, Competence Center Project Governance. Names of the systems have been changed.

4   The Function Point Analysis was performed according to the description of the OMG (OMG/FP 2013)

Since the types of the considered systems are very different, this diagram is helpful to analyze the strengths and weaknesses of the measurement methods. Because the focus is on the relationships between and the courses of the different graphs, figure 11 does not show numerical values on the Y-axis, which has been scaled differently for each method. Systems listed on the left side are relatively small ones with only few use cases. Up to system Himalia, the relationship of the increase measured by the different methods is about the same.

Europa is a real-time system without user interface and database which sends and receives a large number of message types including a total of 22.000 different data elements. For Europa, the functional size measured using the Function Point Analysis was considerably lower than with the other methods.

The systems Io and Callisto are business applications with about 100 masks each and a database with more than 200 tables and about 5.000 attributes. Callisto has masks with a significantly higher complexity than Io. Therefore, the Function Point Analysis and the Data Interaction Point method measure a higher value for Callisto than for Io. However, applying the COSMIC method, results in about the same functional size for Io and Callisto as it does not consider complexity at all.

Ganymede is a part of a banking system. It has about 2.500 masks, a database with more than 30.000 attributes and interfaces with about 20.000 different import/ export attributes in total. The analysis of this very large system was facilitated by machine readable meta information which was the result of a language migration from RPG to Java.

Many large systems, especially older ones, are characterised by masks and database tables, each including a high number of data elements; not to mention the large import and export structures of interfaces. Ganymede is a representative of this class. It is likely that the slight increase of the functional size measured with the Function Point Analysis is due to counting data structures and elementary processes instead of data elements, as the other methods do. This effect is probably being reinforced by determining weights of the objects to be counted by open-ended, three leveled interval scales, where, from a certain size, data structures and elementary processes always have the same weight. All data structures of internal logical files with more than 1 record element type, for example, always have the weight 15 if they include more than 50 data element types. Especially for older systems it is not uncommon that these structures include several hundred data element types. Compared with this, the COSMIC and the Data Interaction Point method count data element types directly, which results in a larger increase of the measured values. Due to the consideration of the complexity by, for example, weighting input fields in masks higher than output fields or persisted elements in database tables higher than those being read only, the values measured by the Data Interaction Point method are higher than those of the COSMIC method.

The results of applying the criteria for assessing measuring methods, which have been described at the beginning of this chapter, are reflected in the following table:

| Objectivity | |
|---|---|
| Function Point Analysis<br>COSMIC Method<br>DIP Method | For all considered methods the measured values are independent of the measuring person – according to the methodical knowledge required. |

| Reliability | |
|---|---|
| Function Point Analysis<br>COSMIC Method<br>DIP Method | All considered methods are counting methods with clearly defined rules. Therefore, repeated measurements of the same object always achieve the same results. |

| Validity | |
|---|---|
| Function Point Analysis | Advantage: The measured results correlate with the functional size as defined by the standard ISO/IEC 14143.<br><br>Disadvantage: From a certain size, the counted data structures and elementary processes always have the same weight. |
| COSMIC Method | Advantage: The measured results correlate with the functional size as defined by the standard ISO/IEC 14143.<br><br>Disadvantage: No consideration of complexity, which can lead to inaccuracy when measuring dialog and database oriented business applications.<br><br>Advantage: Regarding the database, read and write accesses related to the use cases (data movements) are counted instead of its static size.<br><br>The method is well suited for transactional/ real-time applications with less persistence and few dialog related functionalities. |

| DIP Method | Advantage: The measured results correlate with the functional size as defined by the standard ISO/IEC 14143. |
|---|---|
| | Disadvantage: Compared with the COSMIC method which counts data movements, the static consideration of a database bears potential for errors if data elements are counted which are not related to use cases. |
| | Advantage: Allows for adjusting weights according to different system types. Therefore the method is well suited for business applications with a high level of user interactions and for transactional systems as well. |
| **Independency of technological aspects** | |
| Function Point Analysis<br>COSMIC Method<br>DIP Method | All considered methods are independent of technological aspects. |
| **Measurements must be possible before and after the implementation** | |
| Function Point Analysis<br>COSMIC Method<br>DIP Method | All considered methods can be used for measurements prior to the implementation - considering functional specifications - as well as for post-implementation measurements on the basis of structural characteristics of a system. |
| **Economy, ability of automation** | |
| Function Point Analysis<br>COSMIC Method<br>DIP Method | For all considered methods the effort for measuring depends on the quality of available information and on the knowledge about architecture and design of the system to be measured. All methods can be automated if this information is of sufficient quality. |

Table 5: Comparison of FPA, COSMIC and DIP Method

## More measuring methods

There are, of course, more measuring methods which orient themselves more or less towards the functionality of an application instead of its code. Some of them are listed below - without any claim to be exhaustive:

- Data Point Method, Sneed, 1989. Counts tables, keys, relationships and attributes within the database and their use in dialogs and interfaces. Weights are estimated.

- Use Case Point Method, Karner, 1993. Counts use cases and actors. Weights are derived from three-leveled interval scales.

- NESMA Function Point Method (ISO/IEC 24570), The Netherlands Software Metrics users Association (NESMA), 2005. Includes an approximation method and the method "Detailed FPC" which is identical to the original Function Point Analysis.

- Object Point Method, Sneed, 1994. Counts classes, processes and messages on the basis of a class model.

- Bang Metric, De Marco, 1982. Counts functional primitives based on a structured analysis. Weights are derived from the number of input and output tokens.

- FISMA Function Point Method (ISO/IEC 29881), Finnish Software Measurement Association (FiSMA), 2009. Counts data elements crossing the system boundaries, their algorithmic use and read/write accesses to the database. Weights are derived from the type of use.

- Mark II FPA Method (ISO/IEC 20968), United Kingdom Software Metrics Association (UKSMA), 1998. Based on the Function Point Analysis. Counts elementary processes and accesses to the database with specified weights.

It is of primary importance that an organisation performs measurements at all and that it has sufficient method knowledge. As far as the portfolio of own IT systems requires it, one has to make sure that the considered method is suitable for large systems, is able to process logic of heterogeneous complexity, or that measurements can be automated easily.

# V. Automation and the Limits of Measurability

## Measurements are a cross-sectional task

There must be an acceptable relationship between the effort required for software development on the one hand and time and costs of related measurements on the other hand. Otherwise there is the risk that regular measurements will be neglected. But these are crucial for planning the effort and delivery milestones of future development projects reliably and for detecting changes of the productivity, whether caused by improvement measures or by upcoming problems, which require deeper analyses and possibly control measures. It can serve as a benchmark that the size measurement of a large system with several hundreds of dialogs should not require more than 2 days. Due to the usually high work load of staff working in development projects, it makes sense to let employees who are not part of the project perform the measurements. This would also have the advantage that measurement experts can acquire method know-how and expertise concerning automated measurements which can then be applied to other projects of the enterprise.

## Approaches for automated measurements

It is not a desirable task to count objects of an IT application manually. Therefore, measurement experts should aim for automated counting mechanisms. This requires a good knowledge of the application design and of scripts or programs for counting the equivalents of the relevant data elements within the sourcecode, meta data or application models. Some examples of such approaches are listed below:

- GUI frameworks often use models or templates of the dialogs. Technically, these are XML or XHTML files where the usage of tags representing specific GUI elements can be counted.

- If interfaces are based on XML schemes or WSDL files (Web Services Description Language), these files can also be used for counting tags or elements. However, it must be considered that not all data elements defined by a scheme must necessarily be involved in the implemented use cases and their scope. Measuring the functional size of a system requires counting the data elements involved in the functional processes of use cases, not the unused elements which are, for example, embedded in an imported data structure but not processed any further.

- In most DBMS (Database Management Systems), meta data such as the names of tables, attributes and relations of a database can be read from system tables and analyzed by a program.

Even if the effort for implementing a counting program is higher than manual counting, this more than pays off when subsequent measurements can be executed "by the push of a button". However, it must be taken into account that measurements of the functional size, which are based on structural characteristics of an implemented system (e. g. source code patterns) instead of use cases, can lead to inaccuracies.

## Potential inaccuracies when measuring implemented systems

According to the standard ISO/IEC 14143 functional size measurement considers solely the elementary processes of use cases and must be independent of technical and non-functional aspects. In practice, this often conflicts with the call for economy when, for example, the documentation of a banking system's use cases on the level of elementary processes is not available, because its creation is very time-consuming and, therefore, has been neglected in the past. If use cases are not available, an alternative is using structural characteristics of an already implemented system (such as source code, models, meta data – as described in the previous chapter) instead, which represent the objects to be counted. Often automated measurements are not possible otherwise.

Any mapping of use cases on structural characteristics is influenced by the system's design and its degree of re-usability. A dialog may serve as an example, which is involved in multiple use cases of systems A and B. In system A, it has been implemented only once, so, that its functionality is being controlled by the business logic to fit the needs of all use cases. In system B the dialog has been implemented multiple times (adapted to each use case) or the developers have made copies of an already implemented dialog and modified the copies according to the specific use cases. A program for automated size measurements, which counts dialogs or dialog elements, results in a lower size value in the case of system A, where the dialog has been implemented only once and re-used multiple times - compared with system B, where multiple instances of the dialog exist. According to ISO/IEC 14143 this is incorrect if the use cases of both systems are the same. Hence, size measurement on the basis of structural characteristics measures the size of a particular implementation and not the actual use cases.

When comparing size measurements of different systems or derived metrics such as productivity, these differences can be significant. A good indicator for a programming style practicing the re-use of code structures is the ratio between calls and definitions of methods or rather procedures or subroutines, which are implementations of business logic:

$$i_{Re\text{-}use} = \frac{\text{Number of Method Calls}}{\text{Number of Method Definitions}}$$

A ratio of one shows that each method is being called only once in the overall code. The higher the value, the more methods will be called multiple times, which probably reduces the number of redundantly implemented methods. Experience shows that the bandwith of this ratio is from 2,5 to 10. Therefore, measurements of the functional size, which have been made on the basis of structural characteristics and where the measured systems have a different degree of re-usability, are of limited comparability. Due to the observed bandwith of iRe-use, the supposed functional size of systems with exactly the same use cases can differ by a factor of 4 if it has been measured this way.

This effect can have a strong impact on benchmarks of heterogeneous systems if their design and in particular their degree of re-usability is different. It can merely be neglected if measurements of the lifecycle of single systems are compared. However, everybody performing measurements on basis of structural characteristics should be aware of the potential discrepancies compared to the ideal case of using elementary processes of the use cases. A good estimation of these discrepancies can be important, for example, for estimating a risk surcharge on a cost estimation.

# VI. The Impact of Complexity

Almost all known functional size metrics have a problem with considering complexity. The COSMIC method generally does not consider complexity and counts all data movements with the same weight. Although the complexity of interactions levels along with an increasing number, an inaccuracy remains if measurements are taken in one dimension only, that is, when the number of objects will be considered and not their complexity. It seems questionable to ignore complexity, but the dilemma is that there are different types of complexity and their appropriateness for size measurement is not clear at first glance.

## The complexity of implemented code

There are numerous metrics rating aspects of the complexity of implemented code. One of the best-known has been created by Thomas J. McCabe in 1976. It measures the cyclomatic complexity of a program, that is, the number of conditional branches of its control flow graph [McCabe 1976]. This is equal to the number of binary decisions plus 1. Therefore, the cyclomatic complexity can be measured by counting all statements which create new paths within the control flow graph such as „if", iteration constructs, logical operators, and so on.

Figures 12 and 13 give an example of how the cyclomatic complexity of different implementations of the same use case can vary. Both programs are an implementation of the requirement "calculate the product of two integers a and b". The program of figure 12 has a cyclomatic complexity of 1 while the program of figure 13 has a value of 6 (base value 1 plus 3 "if" statements plus 2 loops). As absurd as the approach of figure 13 may be – practical experience shows that the complexity of the implementation of a functional requirement not always achieves the lowest ideal value, because it depends, for example, on the programmer's skill, experience and his/her knowledge of the programming language.

```
c = a * b
```

Figure 12: Sample program #1

```
If b = 0 Then
      c = 0
ElseIf b > 0 Then
      c = 0
      For i = 1 To b
            c = c + a
      Next i
ElseIf b < 0 Then
      b = Abs(b)
      c = 0
      For i = 1 To b
            c = c + a
      Next i
      c = -1 * c
End If
```

Figure 13: Sample Program #2

Another approach for measuring complexity is the metric created by Maurice Halstead in 1977, which rates the lexical/ textual complexity of program code on the basis of a vocabulary, that is, the set of used operands and operators [Halstead 1977]. A further example is the metric „Response for a Class" (RfC), which derives the complexity of a class from its number of methods and the coupling with other classes [ITWissen 2014].

A main characteristic of these metrics is that they measure the complexity of a particular implementation. As the example of figures 12 and 13 indicate there can be almost any number of different implementations of the same functional requirement, each with a different degree of complexity.

Metrics for rating the complexity of a specific implementation are important within the context of maintainability and testability, when related to exactly one particular implementation. However, it is important to keep in mind that another development team would probably have implemented the same requirements differently, resulting in a different rating of maintainability, testability, and so on. For productivity measurements this dependency on individual programming styles or characteristics of a programming language is not desireable because it leads to a restricted validity: A project implementing the same requirements by a larger quantity of circuitous code, with inappropriate complexity and poor modularization and reusability, would probably be honored by a higher productivity rate because it would produce more output with the same effort. But this nullifies the productivity concept as it has been defined in chapter III and it bears the risk that measures planned for improving the productivity promote poor code quality instead.

## Interaction complexity

Functional size metrics measure the size related to interactions between a system and actors of its use cases (functional users). Therefore they should consider the complexity of these interactions, or rather of the functional processes triggered by interactions instead of the complexity of a particular implementation.

The Function Point Analysis takes account of the complexity by counting elementary processes and data structures crossing the system boundaries with different weights. As described before, the weight of an object to be counted is derived from the number of related data elements or structures, which undoubtly serves as a metric for the interaction complexity. The determination of these weights by three-leveled, open-ended, interval scales can lead to inaccuracies with consequences as shown at the end of chapter IV.

A different approach is to derive the complexity from the data movements, as applied by the Data Interaction Point Method. Due to the required validations and persistence, the input of a data element within a dialog is characterised by a higher complexity than its output, which results in a higher weight of this object. Furthermore, writing a data element to the database with all necessary validations, consistency and integrity checks is more complex than read-only access. The advantage of this approach is its unambiguousness. Data elements used for input can be clearly distinguished from those used only for output, even if the counting process has been automated. Additionally, the number of counted input and counted output elements directly affects the measured value – and not by transformations with interval scales as in the case of the Function Point Analysis.

In case of interfaces between the measured and an external system the differentiation of the weights can be difficult. The question whether input or output processing of interfaces is more complex cannot be answered generally. In the best case, complexity classes of different, clearly distinguishable interface types can be defined with weights for all related objects to be counted, which correlate with the complexity of the pre- or post-processing.

Generally, it would be wrong to estimate the interaction complexity of each single object to be counted independently, because different persons can come up with different results, which – after summing up many estimated weights – would reduce the objectivity of the measurement method.

# Algorithmic complexity

In cases where interactions of a system with users or external systems play a dominant role, it makes sense to use a functional size metric which is compliant to ISO/IEC 14143. As described before, these metrics only consider measuring data movements between the system and the actors of use cases.

For systems, which primarily access algorithms and where interactions with actors are only of subordinate importance, functional size metrics as described in this book are not suitable or even unusable. This becomes obvious when looking at a route planning software. Interactions are limited to the input of a start and of one or more destination adresses and as an output you get a list of route sections. Using an ISO/IEC 14143 compliant size metric would result in a low size value for this software and, in case of a productivity measurement, lead to the impression of a low productivity of the software development process. The highly complex planning algorithms would not have been considered, although their implementation had taken an enormous amount of time and effort.

This example of a route planning software shows that measuring the functional size as described by ISO/IEC 14143, gives an incomplete picture of the output of a software development process if a system is characterised by an above-average level of algorithmic complexity. How size and productivity in case of such systems can be measured practically, objectively, reliably and validly, according to the requirements described in chapter IV, has to remain open, because this issue requires further research and investigation. A good practice, which can be recommended, is to separate system components with high algorithmic complexity, measure the rest of the system with a functional size metric and handle the separated part in a different way, for example, by an expert estimation.

# VII. Tips and Hints for the Introduction of regular Productivity Measurements

# Definition of objectives

The amount of time and effort required for the introduction of a measurement method and the regular measurements and analyses should not be underestimated. An organization should be clearly aware of its intended objectives, the requirements and the attainable benefits.

| Objective | Requirements | Benefit |
|---|---|---|
| Reliable planning of new development projects | Regular productivity measurements using the same valid measuring method | Less or no missed deadlines or exceeded budgets |
| Improving productivity | Benchmarks of productivity measurements between different organizational units | Saving of development time and costs |
| Improving quality | Introduction of regular quality measurements and benchmarks between different organizational units | Saving of development time and costs |

Table 6: Relationship of objectives, requirements and benefits

The objectives listed in table 6 cannot be achieved immediately after the introduction of a measurement method. Similar to development projects, such a project requires particular stages of planning and management which will be roughly described in the following chapters.

## Stage 1: Evaluation and calibration of a measuring method

An organization attempting to regularly measure and improve its productivity has to choose for a measurement method sutable for its own systems. The question must be: Are the systems primarily interacting with users and other systems or devices, or is their main purpose the processing of complex algorithms? For the first case chapter IV of this book gives a good orientation and describes pros and cons of different functional size metrics. In case of high algorithmic complexity an easy-to-follow recommendation is not yet possible. However, splitting the systems into a part which can be measured by functional metrics and a part which requires expert estimations could be a possible recommendation.

Regarding the organization's decision for a measuring method, it should be taken into account that the most publicized method is not automatically the best choice. Estimations without clear rules must be avoided. Only counting objects according to clearly defined rules leads to valid mesurements. Sometimes adjustments of the weights can be helpful to fit different interaction types (inputs to and outputs from dialogs and interfaces, database accesses, and so on) to the complexity of the pre- or post-processing, at the price of limited comparability between the concerned systems.

In the later practice, a new measurement must be performed after each new release or increment. To reduce the effort for these regular measurements, the ability of a measuring method to perform automated measurements should be evaluated in detail. This not only requires good expertise of the measuring method, but also in-depth knowledge of the application design and the used software development processes and methods. When automating measurements, possible limitations regarding the comparability of different systems as described in chapter V should be considered.

If a decision for a specific measuring method has been made, the counting rules must be defined precisely. These rules can relate to the characteristics of the systems measured and must describe, which types of objects in which categories have to be counted and which don't. These rules must be strict enough to prevent any personal freedom of interpretation, which could be used by managers to maximize the development output, thereby casting a positive light on their costs.

This stage of evaluation and calibration is completed if measures verify that the requirements on a size metric which have been described at the beginning of chapter IV have been met. Attention should be paid to the fact that any subsequent change of the measuring method can lead to a loss of comparability with previous measurements.

## Stage 2: Launch and collection of empirical values

The objectives listed in table 6 can only be achieved if a sufficient number of values is available, and has been measured by applying consistently the same method. Depending on the frequency of new development projects or release cycles, this stage can take from half a year up to two years.

Apart from the collection of empirical values, which are essential for determining the expected expenses of planned development activities, knowledge building is an important objective of this stage. All parties concerned should understand the basics of measurement, the applied methods and the rules. To achieve this, knowledge must be available in explicit form for every involved employee, trainings must be provided and experts, who can answer questions or clarify issues quickly and competently, must be available. It should be considered that softwaremetry is of little or no importance for many programs of information science, so that the development of fundamental knowledge as well as basic mathematical skills are necessary to ensure that measurements will be understood and accepted.

Another objective of this stage is to organize that the total work performance of all employees involved in the software development process can be determined accurately and reliably – as it has been described in chapter III. This is a mandatory requirement for measuring productivity at all.

For the documentation of measurements standardised templates must be created, which are required to make measurements traceable. The traceability can be supported by unambiguous references to the applied rules and the counted objects within the documentation.

## Stage 3: The practical use of measurements

Only a sufficient number of measurements is suitable for determining the expected expenses of planned development activities and for establishing a continuous improvement process regarding productivity and quality. It makes sense to determine development expenses ex-ante on the basis of the already measured values as early as in stage 2, but to look at these figures with a certain amount of scepticism. After each development activity is completed, the necessary staff effort shows the actual reliability of the method. In case of discrepancies, more empirical values must be collected or it might be necessary to calibrate the measuring method (as described for stage 1).

With the beginning of the practical use of measurements an organization should introduce a management system to promote the goal of increasing productivity systematically. In addition to the measuring methods itself, cycles should be defined for their application, for obtaining key performance indicators, their interpretation and the resulting identification of improvement measures as well as for assessing their implementation according to cost and benefit aspects. This is the objective of the second book of this series with the subtitle "Management Model, Cost Estimation and KPI Improvement".

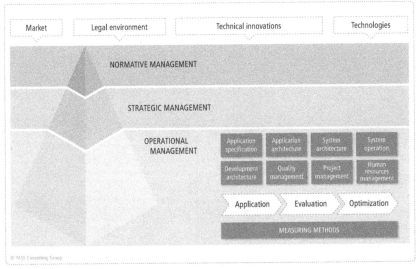

Figure 14: Management Model for Increasing Productivity of Software Development

# VIII. Conclusion

The invention of the steam engine initiated an industrial revolution which changed our world significantly. Strong economic growth was the consequence. After a number of years the delivery of raw materials as well as the distribution of industrially manufactured products reached their limits due to the poor transport facilities at the time. A downswing followed. Then the invention of the railroad together with a transnational rail network, enabling reliable transportation over long distances, supported a new economic upswing. A few years later, new restrictions came up, causing a further downswing, but new important innovations lead to the next upswing. The latest innovation of this cyclic development is the internet. It enables anyone to enter global markets, but at the price of global competition regarding innovation and time: prices, product specifications and performance data, delivery times, ratings by other customers, and so on, can be compared globally. Customers notice any changes of the competitors' offerings immediately, and therefore, vendors who want to remain competitive, are in a tight spot. Successful companies can offer their products to the right target groups at the right time and in an attractive way. They do not waste their customer's valuable time for purchase and payment handling and they can ensure, that a product is delivered almost at the same time the customer clicks the "buy now" button. In other words: the competitive position of companies today depends on their ability to implement new ideas and innovations as quickly as possible by means of IT solutions, that is, software.

One expects software developing enterprises to have short development cycles and reliable planning. Standardization, re-use and automation are proven methods to reduce the development effort. However, many companies still estimate cost and effort of their IT projects and control them by "managing the consumption", in other words, by solely monitoring the residual budget. But for a reliable planning of development projects a method for measuring the size of the software to be produced is needed on the one hand and a precise knowledge of the own productivity (efficiency), which can only be obtained by regular measurements of completed development projects, is needed on the other hand.

Since the 70s, many size metrics have been developed. For systems with a focus on interactions with users or other systems the standard ISO/IEC 14143 is well-proven. Metrics which are compliant to this standard consider use cases or functional requirements and count related data structures or elements, which can be exchanged between the system to be measured and its actors (users as well as other systems). Distinguishing features of today's functional metrics are the practice of counting instead of pure estimations, the use of interval scales or approximation methods as well as the consideration of interactional complexity.

Empirical values of the own productivity as needed for effort estimations of planned development projects cannot be available immediately after the launch of a measuring method. Subsequent productivity measurements of as many completed development projects as possible are required. This means measurements of the software size (the output of the development process) and of the expended man days (its input).

Additionally, increased planning reliability, regular productivity and quality measurements allow benchmarks between different organizational units, help to identify a need for action where the measured productivity is lower than a baseline and show the effectiveness of improvement measures. Deployed correctly, this is the key for the continuous and sustainable improvement of the own software development. The description of a corresponding management model is the subject of the second book of this series.

# Glossary

## Actor

User or external system interacting with a target system in the context of a →use case.

## Agile Development

Type of development characterized by →incremental development, improvements achieved by learning of individuals as well as of the organization, and a close collaboration between all related parties.

## Algorithm

Finite sequence of executable instructions to solve a problem.

## Algorithmic Complexity

Complexity of the program logic implemented in an application.

## Application Architecture

Also: Application design, software architecture or software design. Definition of an application's internal construction by components, their responsibilities, interfaces and communication.

## Base Functional Component

Also: BFC. Step of a →Use case. According to →ISO/IEC 14143, BFCs are the basis of the →Functional size measurement.

## Baseline

In project management, the initial plan used for measuring the project progress. In IT controlling, the reference value in a →benchmark.

### Benchmark

Comparative analysis of metrics or processes with a target value (also: →baseline) or with a reference process.

### Cloud

Also: Cloud computing. →Virtualization of IT infra-structure and its provision via the internet.

### Code Metric

Method for measuring the software size on the basis of characteristics of the source code.

### Complexity

In software development complexity means the effort required to understand a program or →algorithm.

### Component

Capsulated and reusable software unit providing services via well-defined interfaces which can be combined and executed unchanged with other components.

### Continuous Improvement Process

A process of steady, small steps of improvement. In IT, this means a repetitive cycle of the identification of potential improvements on the basis of →root cause analyses and →benchmarks, the respective planning, implementation and a check of the effectiveness.

## COSMIC

Common Software Measurement International Consortium, an international grouping of software measurement experts with the objective of promoting and disseminating the →COSMIC method.

## COSMIC Method

Also: →Full Function Points Method. Method for measuring the size of software by counting data movements related to →use cases. Standardized by the norm →ISO/IEC 19761.

## Cyclomatic Complexity

Also: McCabe metric. →Complexity of a concrete implementation, based on the number of independent branches of the program flowchart. Developed in 1976 by Thomas J. McCabe.

## Data Interaction Point Method

Also: DIP method. Method for measuring the size of software by counting interactions between →actors and a considered system related to →use cases.

## Defect

Also: Bug. Nonfulfillment of or non-compliance with an →explicit or →implicit requirement.

## Defect Density

Indicator of a system's →quality. Calculated from the number of →defects in a particular time range in relation to the system's size.

### Delivery Productivity

→Productivity related to the effective size of a system as delivered to the customer and therefore also including re-used components.

### Delphi Method

Extended expert estimate, where the subject matter is being assessed with finest granularity on the basis of the estimators' experience. It is characterized by a formalized process that involves multiple experts and a moderator.

### Dynamic Baseline

Target value of a →benchmark, which has been derived by the values to be compared, for example, by calculating the average or median of these values.

### Economy

In software development the minimization of duration and costs for systems or processes.

### Effectiveness

Relationship of the objective reached to the objective defined.

### Efficiency

Considers the profitability of a production process in terms of a cost-benefit ratio. In software development processes, it is defined as the ratio of output to input.

### Elementary Process

Another name for a →base functional component as defined by →ISO/IEC 14143.

**EN ISO 9000**

Family of standards defining principles of quality management.

**Expert Estimation**

Effort estimation of multiple persons on the basis of their experiences and by comparing with already performed similar development tasks.

**Explicit Requirement**

Requirement which has been agreed on explicitly with the customer or product owner and has been documented comprehensibly.

**External Benchmark**

→Benchmark for the comparison of own metrics with those of other organisations.

**Full Function Points Method**

Also: FFP method. Original name of the →COSMIC method.

**Function Point Analysis**

Also: FPA. Method for measuring the size of software by counting →elementary processes and data structures related to →use cases. Standardized by the norm →ISO/IEC 20926.

**Functional Requirement**

Also: Functional User Requirement, FUR. Specifies a desired behavior of the running system related to its →use cases.

### Functional Size Measurement

Also: FSM. Method for measuring the size of software on basis of →functional requirements. Standardized by the norm →ISO/IEC 14143

### Functional User

Extended definition of an →actor. A functional user can be a human user, an external system or any input or output device.

### Further Development Productivity

→Productivity of the process for the further development of an existing system.

### IFPUG

Abbreviation for the International Function Point Users Group, a non-profit world-wide organization for the standardization and promotion of the →function point analysis.

### Implicit Requirement

Common expectation regarding a non-functional characteristics where the requirement has not been →explicitely agreed on and documented.

### Incremental Development

Type of software development where parts of a system are developed at different times and the system is extended by already completed parts.

### Individual Software

Software, which has been created to fulfil the specific requirements of a particular customer.

### Industrial Software Development

Software development using methods of the industrial production, in particular standardization, and reuse, automation and performance as well as quality measurements.

### Innovation

The economic implementation of a product or service based on a new idea or invention.

### Innovation Competition

Impact of the market dynamics caused by the internet where companies stand out from the crowd of competitors primariliy due to innovations.

### Interactional Complexity

Complexity of →use case related interactions of →actors with a considered system.

### Internal Benchmark

→Benchmark for the comparison of metrics coming from entities of the own organisation.

### Interval Scale

Metric scale where different levels are defined by intervals of measurements.

### ISO/IEC 14143

Standard for →functional size measurement

**ISO/IEC 19761**

Standard for →COSMIC method

**ISO/IEC 20926**

Standard for →function point analysis

**ISO/IEC 25010**

Standard for software quality. Defines software quality characteristics and their partition into sub-characteristics. Formerly: ISO/IEC 9126.

**Iterative Development**

Step-by-step refinement of implementing requirements, often starting with sophisticated and risky requirements and approximating the system closer to the objective with each iteration.

**Key Performance Area**

Also: KPA. Area with an impact on a specific process or product characteristics. The targeted improvement of a →key performance indicator requires knowledge of the KPAs which have a strong impact on KPIs.

**Key Performance Indicator**

Also: KPI. In the context of IT management the resulting value of a method measuring the progress of a process or product characteristics.

### Knowledge Work

Type of work which requires knowledge to be successful. This can be by knowledge already acquired by the worker (implicit knowledge), new knowledge which the worker learns specially for his task, or explicit knowledge which the worker researchs or which will be provided by a knowledge management process.

### Kondratiev Cycles

Cycles of the economic development which are, according to a model of the economist Nikolai Kondratiev, triggered by →innovations.

### Line-of-Code Metric

→Size metric counting lines of the source code.

### Maintainability

Criteria for the success and effort of changes. There are metrics which can be used as an indicator for the maintainability of a system. Poor maintainability has an impact on →further development productivity.

### Management Model

Schema for implementing a →management system.

### Management System

Framework for management tasks within a particular context including methods for monitoring and controlling the achievment of objectives.

## Metric

In this context: Software metric. Function for mapping a specific process or product characteristics to a numerical value.

## Milestone

A specific date of special significance within a development process. Usually the completion or delivery date of a specific artefact.

## Milestone Trend Analysis

Also: MTA. Specific →milestones of the project plan are tracked over a longer period. From the trend of their postponements the probability of postponements of other milestones will be derived.

## New Development Productivity

→Productivity of the process for the development of a new system.

## Non-functional Requirement

Also: Non-functional User Requirement, NFUR. Specifies the expected characteristics of a product according to →ISO/IEC 25010.

## Object Management Group

Also: OMG. Consortium for the development and maintenance of standards for vendor-independent, object-oriented modeling [OMG 2015].

## Objectivity

A →metric is objective if the measured values are independent of the measuring person.

### Persistence

Ability of a system to keep data (objects, states) or logical connections over a long period, in particular beyond a program abortion.

### Process Metric

A →metric for measuring a characteristic of a process. →Productivity is a process metric for measuring the →efficiency.

### Productivity

A →process metric. In software development →efficiency is usually considered as productivity.

### Quality

Degree of fulfilment of →explicit and →implicit requirements.

### Quality Assurance, analytical

Generic term for all activities related to searching, fixing and tracking →defects.

### Quality Assurance, constructive

Generic term for all activities related to preventing →defects, for example by pre-defind processes, methods, guidelines, tools, and so on.

### Quality Assurance, organizational

Generic term for the support of quality by expert roles and panels, for example, business or technical committees, security experts, subject matter experts, controlling boards or a steering committee.

### Quality Characteristic

Property of →quality. The standard →ISO/IEC 25010 describes software quality characteristics.

### Quality Gate

A →milestone in the course of a project where continuation or completion depends on the compliance with defined quality criteria.

### Redesign

Structural improvement of the →Application Architecture without changes of the functionality.

### Refactoring

Structural improvement of the code without changes of the functionality.

### Release

New version of an application.

### Reliability

A →metric is reliable if repeated measurements of the same object always come to the same result.

### Return on Investment

Also: RoI. Model for the determination of the return of an entrepreneurial activity on the basis of the relationship of profit and invested capital.

## Root Cause Analysis

Method for identifying the cause at the beginning of a cause-effect chain of a →defect.

## Size Metric

A →metric for measuring the size of an IT system. Depending on the measuring method, the result can refer to the functional size, the program length, and so on.

## Standard Software

Contrary to →individual software, standard software fulfills uniform requirements of numerous customers.

## System Architecture

Definition of a system's internal construction by components such as applications, interfaces, database management systems, application servers, and so on.

## Technical Debt

Negligence in the new development of a system. Impacts are insufficient →maintainability and poor →further development productivity.

## Test Automation

Automated execution of test cases. Possible with unit tests, end-to-end tests and load tests.

## Test Coverage

A →metric for measuring the percentage of →elementary processes, branches of the program flowchart, code lines, and so on which have been checked for →defects.

## Time-based Competition

Also: TBC. The focus of providers of products and services in the internet on the time until the market entry (time to market) as a strategic competitive advantage.

## Time Gap

The dilemma caused by the market dynamics in the internet (→time-based competition) on one side and the increasing complexity of new products and services that give competitive advantages on the other side.

## Use Case

Use cases describe all scenarios of how →actors can accomplish specific goals by using a considered system. Each use case is defined by →elementary processes defining interactions between actors and the system abstracted from specific technical solutions [Cockburn 2002].

## Validity

A →metric is valid, if the measured values represent the characteristics to be measured.

## Virtualization

Simulation of a physical object or a resource using IT.

# Bibliography

**Alex 1997** J. Alex (1997): „Wege und Irrwege des Konrad Zuse". Spektrum der Wissenschaft 1/1997: 78.

**Cockburn 2002** Alistair Cockburn (2002): „Use cases, ten years later". URL http://a.cockburn.us/2098 (11.02.2015).

**Cohen/Schmidt 2013** Jared Cohen/ Eric Schmidt (2013): „The New Digital Age: Reshaping the Future of People, Nations and Business". John Murray Publishers.

**COSMIC 2015** COSMIC (2015): Website of the Common Software Measurement International Consortium. URL http://www.cosmicon.com (11.02.2015).

**COSMIC FSM 2014** COSMIC FSM (2014): „The COSMIC Functional Size Measurement Method Version 4.0; Measurement Manual; The COSMIC Implementation Guide for ISO/IEC 19761:2011".URL http://www.cosmicon.com/portal/public/MM4.pdf (11.02.12015).

**Grönroos/Ojasalo 2002** Christian Grönroos/Katri Ojasalo (2002): „Service productivity - Towards a conceptualization of the transformation of inputs into economic results in services". Journal of Business Research 57 (2004): 414–423. URL http://ipam5ever.com.sapo.pt/profile/Service%20Productivity%20JBR.pdf (02.05.2014).

**Halstead 1977** Maurice Howard Halstead (1977): „Elements of Software Science (Operating and programming systems series)". Elsevier Science Ltd., New York.

**ISO/IEC 14143 2007** ISO/IEC 14143-1:2007 (2007): „Information technology -- Software measurement -- Functional size measurement -- Part 1: Definition of concepts". ISO (International Organization for Standardization).

**ISO/IEC 20926 2009** ISO/IEC 20926:2009 (2009): „Software and systems engineering -- Software measurement -- IFPUG functional size measurement method 2009". ISO (International Organization for Standardization).

**ITWissen 2014** ITWissen (2014): „Das große Online-Lexikon für Informationstechnologie: RFC (response for a class)". URL http://www.itwissen. info/definition/lexikon/RFC-response-for-a-class.html (02.05.2014).

**Korotayev/Tsirel 2010** Korotayev, Andrey V./ Tsirel, Sergey V. (2010): „A Spectral Analysis of World GDP Dynamics: Kondratiev Waves, Kuznets Swings, Juglar and Kitchin Cycles in Global Economic Development, and the 2008–2009 Economic Crisis". Structure and Dynamics 4/2010 (1): 3–57.

**Lanier 2014** Jaron Lanier (2014): „Wem gehört die Zukunft?: Du bist nicht der Kunde der Internetkonzerne. Du bist ihr Produkt". Hoffmann und Campe Verlag.

**McCabe 1976** Thomas J. McCabe (1976): „A Complexity Measure". IEEE Transactions on Software Engineering, SE-2 (4), Dec 1976. URL http://www. literateprogramming.com/mccabe.pdf (11.02.2015).

**Meister 2012** Ulrich Meister (2012): „Vision 2030: So leben, arbeiten und kommunizieren wir im Jahr 2030". Verlag GABAL.

**Moore 1998** Gordon E. Moore (1998): „Cramming More Components onto Integrated Circuits". Proceedings of the IEEE 86 (1). URL http://www.cs.utexas.edu/~fussell/courses/cs352h/papers/moore.pdf (11.02.2015).

**OMG 2015** OMG (2015): Website of the Object Management Group. URL http://www.omg.org/gettingstarted/gettingstartedindex.htm (12.02.2015).

**OMG/FP 2013** OMG (2013): „Automated Function Points". Object Management Group, Document Number ptc/2013-02-01. URL http://www.omg.org/spec/AFP/1.0/Beta1/PDF (02.05.2014).

**PASS 2013** PASS (2013): „Description of the PASS Data Interaction Point Method (DIP Method)". PASS Consulting Group (unpublished).

**Rienecker et al 2011** Gerhard Rienecker et al (2011): „Quality that's IT - Informationstechnologie als strategisches Mittel im Qualitätswettbewerb". PASS IT-Consulting Dipl.-Inf. G. Rienecker GmbH & Co. KG.

**Rifkin 2011** Jeremy Rifkin (2011): „Die dritte industrielle Revolution: Die Zukunft der Wirtschaft nach dem Atomzeitalter". Campus Verlag.

**Streibich 2014** Karl-Heinz Streibich (2014): „The Digital Enterprise". Software AG.

# About the Author

Stefan Luckhaus is a computer scientist with more than 35 years of experience. He has been working in software development since 1981 and graduated in Frankfurt in 1988, with the academic degree of Dipl.-Ing. (FH). Subsequently, he was a freelancer for 10 years. Since 1998, Stefan Luckhaus has been an employee of PASS Consulting Group. Initially working as a developer, he later managed development projects leading him to the USA, Singapore, India and various European countries. Today, Stefan Luckhaus is responsible for the competence center Project Governance, providing process engineering for the software development of the entire PASS group. Here, he conducts productivity and quality measurements for more than 20 IT shops internally as well as on behalf of customers. He is a member of the PASS group's R&D unit and has the status of a principal innovation consultant.

Stefan Luckhaus' fields of expertise are software metrics, quality management and process models / engineering for software development. In the German ICT industry association BITKOM (Bundesverband Informationswirtschaft, Telekommunikation und neue Medien e.V.) he chairs the work group Quality Management, collaborated in the publication of „Agile Software Engineering Made in Germany" and is a speaker for example at the Bitkom Software Summits.

Stefan Luckhaus is present on the social networks LinkedIn, Xing and Twitter. He authors the blog www.software-productivity.com and co-authors the blog www.travel-industry-blog.com.

# Book Recommendations

Stefan Luckhaus

# Book Series
## Increasing Productivity of Software Development

# Part 2
# Management Model, Cost Estimation and KPI Improvement

Standardization and automation can increase the productivity of software development by a factor of 20 – compared to the development by way of manufacture. If a software manufacture needs 1,000 man days, with this paradigm the development costs for the same product can be reduced to 50 man days. When re-using business and technical components, a factor of 100 could already be measured in practice.

Such differences in performance can only be understood by measurements. This book describes a management model which is based on three key performance indicators (KPIs): productivity (based on labour), costs (based on overall costs) and quality. It explains their cyclic determination using according measurement methods as well as their analytical evaluation. The book also explains indicators, leading to improvements within 8 key performance areas (KPAs) of software development, based on the development of productivity and quality within a certain period of time or on the results of methodical root cause analyses. For assessing the anticipated effectiveness of improvement measures in advance, it provides a calculation method as well as many empirical values.

ISBN

Hardcover:  978-3-9819565-2-8
Paperback:  978-3-9819565-5-9
e-Book:     978-3-9819565-3-5

# Contents

Introduction: Factories – from Manufactures to Software Production

The potential of productivity improvements

The manufacture – handcrafting software

Development standards

Automated production processes

Standardization and re-use of functional components

A management model for optimizing productivity

I. KPIs and measuring methods

Measuring productivity

Measuring quality

Cycles of measurement, evaluation and optimization

II. Application of Measuring Methods

Measuring delivery- and new-development productivity

Measuring further-development productivity

Deriving quality indicators

Calculating the costs of planned development projects

Step 1: Determining the size of functional requirements

Step 2: Finding an empirical value for own productivity

Step 3: Interpreting the result

Step 4: Identifying additional effort

Step 5: Identifying and mitigating risks

III. Evaluation

Analyzing the course of productivity over time

Internal benchmarks

External benchmarks

Reference values

Comparing quality with productivity

Anomaly #1: The impact of neglected analytical quality assurance

Anomaly #2: The impact of technical debts

Root cause analyses

IV. Optimization

Key performance areas

Application specification

Application architecture

System architecture

System operation

Development architecture

Quality management

Project management

Human resources management

Calculating the effectiveness of improvement measures

Justifying and calibrating measuring methods

Conclusion

Stefan Luckhaus

# Cost Estimation in Agile Software Development

## Utilizing Functional Size Measurement Methods

Whenever software is developed based on contracts with binding conditions such as the delivery of a clearly defined functional scope at a fixed price and at an agreed delivery date, it is exposed to risks. Many of these risks can be mitigated by the principles of agile development. Being able to navigate projects within all agreed parameters requires cost estimation methods to be integrated into planning and controlling processes. In order to prevent these methods from eroding the advantages of agile development, they must be rapidly applicable - ideally automatable - and allow for selfcalibration after every sprint.

This book illustrates, how size metrics can be utilised profitably in software development processes oriented towards agile values. It points out differences and restrictions, shows how the accuracy of cost estimations can be increased with each sprint and examines the feasibility of automated measurements.

ISBN

Hardcover:   978-3-7345-4372-2
Paperback:   978-3-7345-4371-5
e-Book:      978-3-7345-4373-9

# Contents

Characteristics and Importance of Agile Software Development

    Genesis

    Status quo

    Reliability

Direct and indirect Cost Estimation Methods

    Principle of incremental development

    Expert estimations

    Indirect estimations with story points

    Indirect estimations by measuring the functional size

    Summary

Methods for Functional Size Measurement

    Function Point Analysis

    COSMIC Method

    Data Interaction Point Method

    Extending methods for measuring the size of further development

    The Impact of complexity

        The complexity of an implementation

        Interactional complexity

        Algorithmic complexity

    Method comparison

    Further methods

Measuring the Reference Value for an indirect Cost Estimation

    Regular measuring of productivity

        Process scope regarding work

        Process scope regarding sub-processes

        Process scope regarding quality

    Automated Measurements

        Mapping of objects to be counted on structural characteristics

        Possible restrictions

    Iterative refinement of the measured productivity

    Considering non-functional requirements

    Regular measurements

        The relationship of productivity and quality

Conclusion